World About Us

Plants

By Margaret Grieveson

Stargazer Books

© Aladdin Books Ltd 2006

Designed and produced by
Aladdin Books Ltd

**First published in the
United States in 2006 by**
Stargazer Books
c/o The Creative Company
123 South Broad Street
P.O. Box 227
Mankato, Minnesota 56002

Printed in Malaysia

Editor:
Harriet Brown

Design:
Flick, Book Design and Graphics

Picture Researchers:
Brian Hunter Smart
Harriet Brown

Literacy consultant:
Jackie Holderness—former
Senior Lecturer in Primary
Education, Westminster Institute
of Education, Oxford Brookes
University, UK.

*Library of Congress Cataloging-in-
Publication Data*

Grieveson, Margaret.
    Plants / by Margaret Grieveson.
    p. cm. -- (World about us)
    Includes index.
    ISBN 1-59604-037-8
    1. Plants--Juvenile literature.
    2. Botany--Juvenile literature.
    I. Title. II. World about us
    (North Mankato, Minn.)

QK49.G6853 2005
580--dc22
                        2004058608

CONTENTS

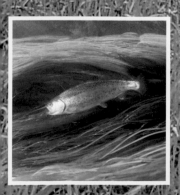

Notes to parents and teachers

This series has been developed for group use in the classroom, as well as for children reading alone. In particular, its text on two levels allows children of mixed abilities to enjoy reading about the same topic. The larger size text (A, below) offers apprentice readers a simplified text. This simplified text is used in the introduction to each chapter and in the picture captions. This font is part of the © Sassoon family of fonts whose maximum legibility is recommended for early readers. The smaller size text (B, below) offers a more challenging read for older or more able readers.

Making new plants

Most plants have flowers so they can make seeds. There is a new plant with a tiny root and shoot inside every seed.

A

◀ Plants need soil, water, and sunlight.

Once a seed has begun to sprout it usually needs soil, water, and sunlight so it can grow.

B

Questions, key words, and glossary

Each spread ends with a question that parents and teachers can use to discuss and develop further ideas and concepts. Further questions are provided in a quiz on page 30. A reduced version of pages 30 and 31 is shown below. The illustrated "Key words" section is provided as a revision tool, particularly for apprentice readers, in order to help with spelling, writing, and guided reading. The glossary is for more able or older readers.

In addition to the glossary's role as a reference aid, it is also designed to reinforce new vocabulary and provide a tool for further discussion and revision. When glossary terms first appear in the text they are highlighted in bold.

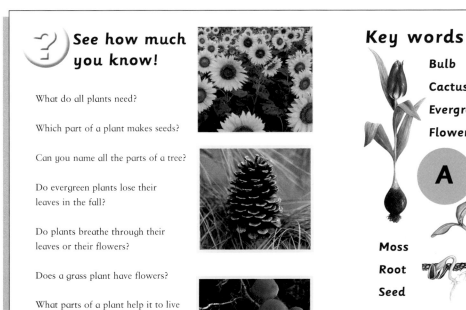

See how much you know!

What do all plants need?

Which part of a plant makes seeds?

Can you name all the parts of a tree?

Do evergreen plants lose their leaves in the fall?

Do plants breathe through their leaves or their flowers?

Does a grass plant have flowers?

What parts of a plant help it to live in a dry place?

Where do lichens grow?

How can plants protect themselves?

Key words

Bulb

Cactus

Evergreen

Flower

A

Moss

Root

Seed

B

Stem

Trunk

Glossary

Absorb—To take something in.
Adapt—The way that something changes to make the best use of a habitat.
Chlorophyll—The green chemical that plants need for photosynthesis.
Deciduous—Trees that lose all their leaves in the fall.
Dormant—Something that is not growing but could do so with the right conditions.
Evergreen—Trees leaves all year
Habitat—The plant or animals
Photosynthesis—The way plants make food using water, air, and sunlight.
Reproduce—The way that plants or animals make new versions of themselves.
Species—A particular kind of plant or animal.

The plant world

Some plants are so small they are hard to see. Some are so big they seem to touch the sky. Plants grow in many places. If you look you will find plants around your home and school, as well as in parks and in the country.

▲
◀ Here are some tiny plants and a very tall tree.

Plants have been on planet Earth for 400 million years. They even existed before dinosaurs! Today, scientists think there are as many as ten million different kinds of plants. Some plants die after a few days and others live for hundreds of years.

Plants come in all shapes and sizes.

Look at the plants below. Two of the plants have colorful flowers. Two plants have no flowers at all. Can you find other ways in which the plants are different from each other?

▲ **Some plants live in very dry places and others live in water.**

Wherever plants grow they make the best use of the light, soil, and water that is there. The place where they grow is called their **habitat**. Each type of plant has a habitat in which it grows best. Waterlilies grow best in fresh water. Cacti grow best where there is a lot of sunlight.

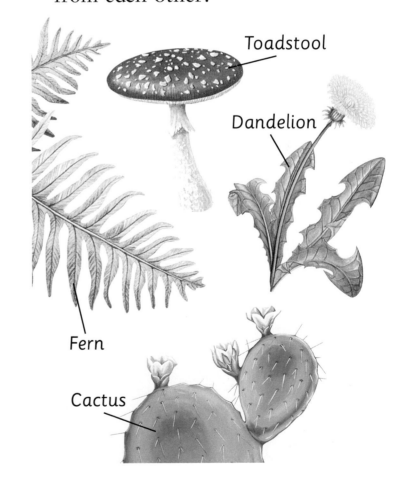

Toadstool

Dandelion

Fern

Cactus

 What is the biggest plant you've ever seen?

Plants are living things

Plants need sunlight, air, and water. Most plants have roots to hold them in the ground and to suck up water. They have stems to hold up their leaves. Most plants have green leaves. They use their leaves to make food.

◀ **This plant has roots, a strong stem, and green leaves.**

All living things, including plants, have seven things in common. They ① feed, ② move, ③ breathe, ④ get rid of waste products, ⑤ grow, ⑥ are sensitive to things like light and heat, and ⑦ they make new versions of themselves.

Most plants have flowers. Seeds are made in the flowers.

Most plants **reproduce** (make new versions of themselves) from seeds. Seeds are made in the flowers. Flowers are often brightly colored and have a strong smell. The seeds of some plants are hidden in their fruits.

Flower

Fruit

Leaves

Stem

Roots

Stems hold the leaves and flowers up to the sun.

The roots, stem, leaves, and flowers are different for each kind of plant. The parts are **adapted** so the plant can have all the sunlight and water it needs. Roots try to find water, and leaves gather sunlight.

What parts do most plants have?

How do plants drink?

All living things need water. Plants drink by sucking up water with their roots. Water travels up the stem to the leaves. If a plant does not have water the stem will flop (see left). The leaves and stem will dry out and the plant will die.

◄ Plants need a little water, but not too much.

If plants do not have water, they dry up and die. Indoor plants need to be watered, but too much water can be bad for them. If they are too wet the plants will rot. A plant's roots have thin "hairs" at the end of them. It is these root hairs that **absorb** water. The main roots then carry the water up to the plant.

▲ **In summer, people may need to water plants that grow outside.**

Plants lose water through their leaves. When the weather is warm and dry, plants lose more water than usual. They need to drink extra water to stay alive. If there is too little rain, gardeners need to water their plants.

See how plants drink! The water travels up the stem to the leaves.

Put a few drops of food coloring into a glass of water. Ask an adult to cut a stick of celery. Put it in the colored water. Look at the celery after 30 minutes. Does the colored water move up the stem toward the leaves? Cut the celery in two. Can you see the tubes holding the water?

Tube carrying water

 What would happen if a plant had no roots?

How do plants breathe?

Most living things need air to live. You cannot see the air, but it is all around you. You can feel it when the wind blows. Animals and plants breathe in and out all the time. Without air they would die. Plants need to breathe so they can make food.

◀ Animals and plants need different parts of the air.

Air is made up of nitrogen, oxygen, and carbon dioxide. Plants take in carbon dioxide. They use the carbon to make food and release oxygen back into the air. Plants do not breathe in and out in the same way as animals. Instead, they absorb carbon dioxide from the air.

▲ Animals need the oxygen that plants give out.

Animals, including humans, need oxygen to survive. Plants give out the oxygen that we need to breathe. Without plants we would not have enough oxygen. This is one reason why it is important to protect forests, especially the huge rainforests of South America.

Plants breathe with their leaves.

There are tiny holes on the underside of each leaf. Plants take in carbon dioxide and give out oxygen through these holes. The holes are called **stomata**.

Stomata are a plant's breathing holes. They are too tiny to see.

 Plants do not have noses, so how do they breathe?

13

How do plants feed?

Plants make their own food. They do this in the green parts of their leaves. Most plants need sunlight to make food, so they grow toward the sun. Plants also need air and water to make their sugary food.

▶ Plants only make food in the daytime when there is light.

To make food in their green leaves plants need water, carbon dioxide, and sunlight. A chemical in leaves called **chlorophyll** absorbs the energy from sunlight. It uses this energy to turn the carbon dioxide and water into sugar. It is chlorophyll that makes leaves look green.

▲ **Sunflowers turn their heads to follow the sun as it crosses the sky.**

Plants compete with each other for light. They angle their leaves and flowers to catch as much sunlight as possible. If there is not enough light, they grow tall and thin.

This picture shows how plants make food.

Plants need sunlight, water, and carbon dioxide to make food. The way plants make their sugary food is called **photosynthesis**.

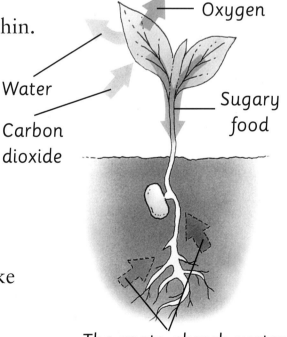

Sun

Oxygen

Water

Carbon dioxide

Sugary food

The roots absorb water.

 What would happen if a plant had no leaves?

Making new plants

Most plants have flowers so they can make seeds. There is a new plant with a tiny root and shoot inside every seed. There is also some food for the new plant in the seed. A seed needs water and light so it can start to grow.

◀ Plants need sunlight, soil, and water to grow.

Once a seed has begun to sprout it usually needs soil, water, and sunlight so it can grow from a seedling into a healthy plant. Some plants make new plants by sending out stems that grow roots and turn into new plants. The shoots they send out are called runners.

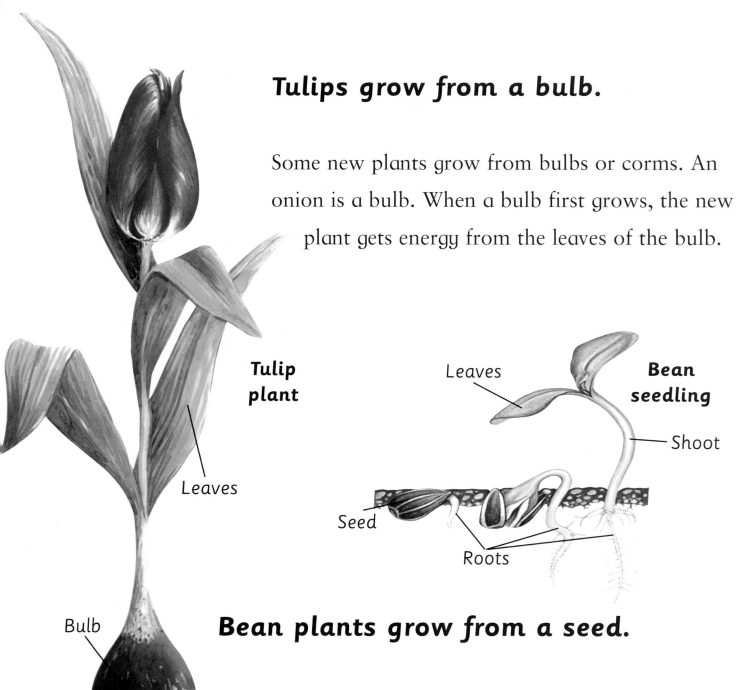

Tulips grow from a bulb.

Some new plants grow from bulbs or corms. An onion is a bulb. When a bulb first grows, the new plant gets energy from the leaves of the bulb.

Tulip plant

Leaves

Bulb

Roots

Leaves

Bean seedling

Shoot

Seed

Roots

Bean plants grow from a seed.

Seeds do not grow until the conditions are right. When a seed finds the right conditions, it will grow a root and a shoot. Some coconut palm seeds float out at sea for months before they reach a place to grow.

 Will a seed grow well in the dark?

Where do plants live?

Plants grow all over the world. They make the best use they can of the soil, water, and sunlight. Where it is hot and wet, the trees grow very tall. Where it is cold and windy, the plants are very small.

▲ **These plants grow on a mountain.**

Alpine plants have small leaves and thick stems to help them survive on a cold, windy mountainside.

▶ **These trees grow in hot, wet places.**

Trees in hot, steamy rainforests must be tall to reach the sunlight.

◀ Seaweed grows in the sea.

Seaweed has adapted to living in saltwater. Some seaweed has pockets filled with air on its leaves. This helps it to float near the surface so that sunlight can reach it.

This plant is growing on another plant.

This is a mistletoe plant. It is growing on an apple tree. It has green leaves so it can make its own food, but it also takes food and water from the tree. It grows high up on the tree so it has plenty of light. Mistletoe does not usually kill the plant it lives on. If the apple tree dies, so does the mistletoe.

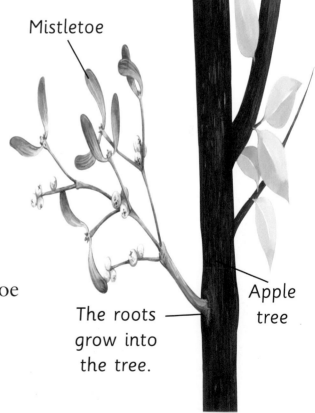

Mistletoe

The roots grow into the tree.

Apple tree

 Can you name some odd places where plants grow?

19

Plant survival

Plants can live almost anywhere. They live in dry deserts. It may not rain there for years. Cactus plants can live in hot deserts. They have thin, sharp leaves, thick skins, and long roots. They suck up water from far under the ground.

◀ This is a very large cactus. It stores water in its thick stem.

Deserts can be cold and dry or hot and dry. Plants can live in both hot and cold deserts, but they have to be very tough. They need a way to store water for a long time. They do this by having a thick stem and skin, and thin spikes instead of broad leaves. Thin leaves lose less water than broad leaves.

▶ Some plants survive in muddy swamps.

Mangrove trees grow along tropical coasts in saltwater. Mangroves have branches that send roots down into the water. Eventually, the stilt-like roots support the leafy tree above the water and hold it safely in place.

Seeds survive for a long time in the dry desert.

When rain falls on a hot desert, plants spring to life. Seeds buried in the sand grow into flowering plants. In just a few weeks they can produce seeds and die back. The seeds lie **dormant** in the ground for many months until the next rains.

 A cactus stores water. Do you know an animal that can?

Trees

Trees are the biggest plants of all. Three are three kinds of trees—palm (left), evergreen, and deciduous trees. The trunk of a tree is covered with bark. You can tell the age of a tree by counting the rings on a tree stump. Some trees can live for 4,000 years!

▶ Some trees keep their leaves all year. They are evergreen.

Most pine and fir trees are **evergreen**. They have cones and are called conifers. Cones are the flowers of the conifer tree. The leaves on conifers are called needles. A few needles drop off every day and new ones grow all year round.

 Some trees lose all their leaves in the fall.

In fall, the weather becomes colder and there are fewer hours of sunshine. This makes the leaves of some trees change color and fall off. Trees that lose all their leaves after they change color in the fall are called **deciduous** trees. Oak and beech trees are deciduous.

Roots grow down to find water.

A tree's roots can spread wider under the ground than the branches spread above the ground.

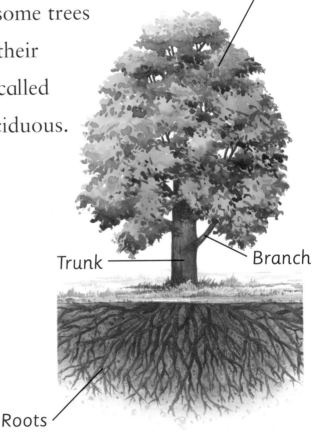

Leaves

Trunk

Branch

Roots

 A coconut is a tree seed. Can you name any others?

Grasses

Grass plants grow all over the world. Some grasses are taller than people, but other kinds of grass only grow a few inches (6-7 cm) high. Grasses have roots, stems, leaves, and flowers. Grasses need sunlight and water to grow well.

◀ **Some animals eat this thick bamboo.**

Bamboo (left) is a very thick, fast-growing grass. Some bamboo can grow two inches (5 cm) in just one hour! There are about 8,000 **species** (types) of grass. Different kinds of grasses grow in different parts of the world. Some grasses or cereal crops, such as wheat, rice, and oats, can give us food.

▲ **Some animals eat grass, but it soon grows again.**

There are huge grasslands in Africa where zebra graze, but grass isn't only used as food. On sand dunes, marram grass is grown to stop the sand from blowing away.

This grass has a very long stem.

Grasses grow quickly when there is enough water. As long as the roots have not been pulled up, grasses can go on growing even when the leaves and stems have been cut or eaten by animals.

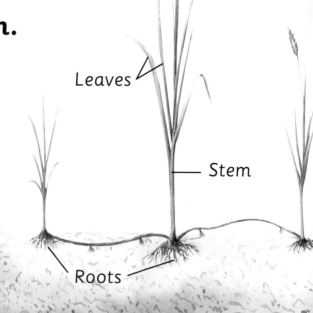

Seeds

Leaves

Stem

Roots

 How are trees and grasses alike?

Moss, lichen, and fungus

Mosses, lichens, and fungi do not have flowers. Without flowers they cannot make seeds. Their new plants grow from spores instead. Mosses, lichens, and fungi do not need to grow in soil. Mosses make their own food. Fungi feed on the dead things they grow on!

▶ A patch of moss is made up of hundreds of tiny moss plants.

Moss can grow on the ground, on rocks, or on rotting logs in cool, damp places. There are nearly 10,000 different species of moss. They are usually small plants but in tropical parts of the world, some mosses can reach 28 inches (71 cm) tall.

◄ Lichens can grow on trees or on rock.

Many tiny lichen plants grow side by side and form larger patches of color. Lichens are made of two types of plants, usually fungi and algae.

► Fungus grows on dead leaves, trees, and old food.

A fungus has no green parts and cannot make its own food. Mushrooms, toadstools, and molds are fungi. Fungi feed off the rotting parts of plants and animals they grow on. Although some of them are edible, it is best to avoid any you come across in the wild. Some toadstools can kill a human.

 Which other plants do not need to grow in soil?

Plant protection

Many plants cannot grow or make seeds if their stems and leaves have been torn off or eaten by an animal. Some plants have leaves that taste bitter. Other plants have thorns, prickles, or sharp leaves to keep them safe.

◀ This plant has thorns to keep animals away.

If plants are to stay alive, they have to protect themselves. Some plants do this by having prickly thorns. Thorns are special short, sharp branches. Other plants, such as holly, protect themselves by having spiny leaves. If an animal tries to eat a spiky plant, it will soon be scared off!

▲ **Some plants are poisonous to stop any animals or people eating them.**

Buttercups (above left) and sweet peas (above right) protect themselves by being poisonous. Eating either of these plants would make you ill.

Nettles sting to protect themselves.

A nettle leaf is covered in tiny hollow spines. If you touch a nettle leaf, the spine breaks off and stabs your skin. A tiny drop of acid enters your skin, making it itch and blister.

A nettle spine

 Can you name three spiky plants?

See how much you know!

What do all plants need?

Which part of a plant makes seeds?

Can you name all the parts of a tree?

Do evergreen plants lose their leaves in fall?

Do plants breathe through their leaves or their flowers?

Does a grass plant have flowers?

What parts of a plant help it to live in a dry place?

Where do lichens grow?

How can plants protect themselves?

Key words

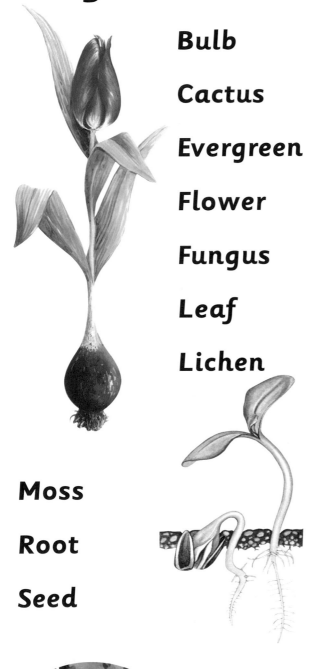

Bulb

Cactus

Evergreen

Flower

Fungus

Leaf

Lichen

Moss

Root

Seed

Stem

Trunk

Glossary

Absorb—To take something in.

Adapt—The way that something changes to make the best use of a habitat.

Chlorophyll—The green chemical that plants need for photosynthesis.

Deciduous—Trees that lose all their leaves in fall.

Dormant—Something that is not growing but could do so with the right conditions.

Evergreen—Trees that keep their leaves all year round.

Habitat—The place in which a plant or animal lives.

Photosynthesis—The way plants make food using water, air, and sunlight.

Reproduce—The way that plants or animals make new versions of themselves.

Species—A particular kind of plant or animal.

Stomata—The tiny holes in leaves through which plants breathe.

Index

Photocredits:
Abbreviations: l-left, r-right, b-bottom, t-top, c-center, m-middle.
Front cover, 5cm, 8bl, 22br, 23t, 30mr— Photodisc. Back cover, 1, 10 both, 14tl, 21tr, 28 both. 29tl—Flick Smith. 2-3, 29tr—Bruce McKenzie. 3tl, 8tr—Scott Bauer/USDA. 3mlt, 7 both, 12tl, 18 both, 20 both, 21mr, 22bm, 24tl—Corel. 3mlb, 13t—John Foxx Images. 3bl, 12bl, 19tl— Stockbyte. 4ml, 14br, 16tl, 25t—Digital Stock. 4bl, 16bl—Comstock. 5ct, 15t, 30tr—Bruce Fritz/USDA. 5cb, 6l, 9tr, 22tl, 24bl, 26 both, 27br, 30br—John Harvey. 6mr—Michael Thompson/USDA. 11tl, 29mr—PBD. 12ml—Bob Nichols/USDA. 27tl—Carol Baldwin/NOAA OMAO. 27tm—Captain Albert E. Theberge/ NOAA Corps.

Step-by-Step Transformations

Turning Wax into Crayons

Herald McKinley

Cavendish Square

New York

Published in 2015 by Cavendish Square Publishing, LLC
243 5th Avenue, Suite 136, New York, NY 10016

Copyright © 2015 by Cavendish Square Publishing, LLC

First Edition

Website: cavendishsq.com

This publication represents the opinions and views of the author based on his or her personal experience, knowledge, and research. The information in this book serves as a general guide only. The author and publisher have used their best efforts in preparing this book and disclaim liability rising directly or indirectly from the use and application of this book.

CPSIA Compliance Information: Batch #WS14CSQ

All websites were available and accurate when this book was sent to press.

Library of Congress Cataloging-in-Publication Data
McKinley, Herald.
Turning wax into crayons / Herald McKinley.
pages cm. — (Step-by-step transformations)
Includes index.
ISBN 978-1-62712-366-2 (hardcover) ISBN 978-1-62712-490-4 (paperback) ISBN 978-1-62713-003-5 (ebook)
1. Crayons—Juvenile literature. 2. Manufacturing processes—Juvenile literature. I. Title.

NC870.M38 2014
741.2'3—dc23

2014001538

Editorial Director: Dean Miller
Editor: Amy Hayes
Copy Editor: Cynthia Roby
Art Director: Jeffrey Talbot
Designer: Joseph Macri
Photo Researcher: J8 Media
Production Manager: Jennifer Ryder-Talbot
Production Editor: David McNamara

The photographs in this book are used by permission and through the courtesy of: Cover photos by AP Photo/Steve Klaver; Tim Perdue/ Flickr Open/Getty Images; © iStockphoto.com/pkdirector, 5; ©The Star-Ledger/Frank Conlon/The Image Works, 7; Photos courtesy Crayola, used with permission. ©2015 Crayola LLC. Crayola® and Serpentine Design® are trademarks of Crayola, 9, 11, 15, 19; William Thomas Cain/Getty Images, 13; AP Photo/Rick Smith, 17; /Blend Images/SuperStock, 21; Back Cover: Derek E. Rothchild/The Image Bank/Getty Images.

Printed in the United States of America

Contents

Crayons are made from **wax.**

4

5

First, the wax is heated.

Wax **melts** when it is hot.

Colored **powder** is mixed
into the hot wax.

The wax becomes the same
color as the powder.

9

Next, the colored wax is poured into a **mold**.

The mold will form the wax into the shape of crayons.

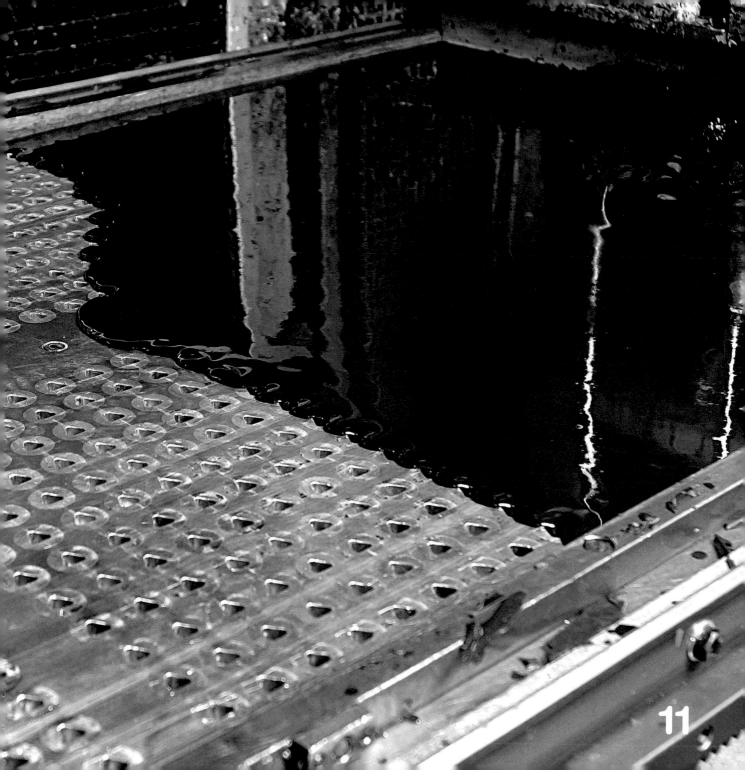

11

As the wax cools, it becomes hard.

The hard wax is taken out of the mold.

The wax is now in the shape of crayons.

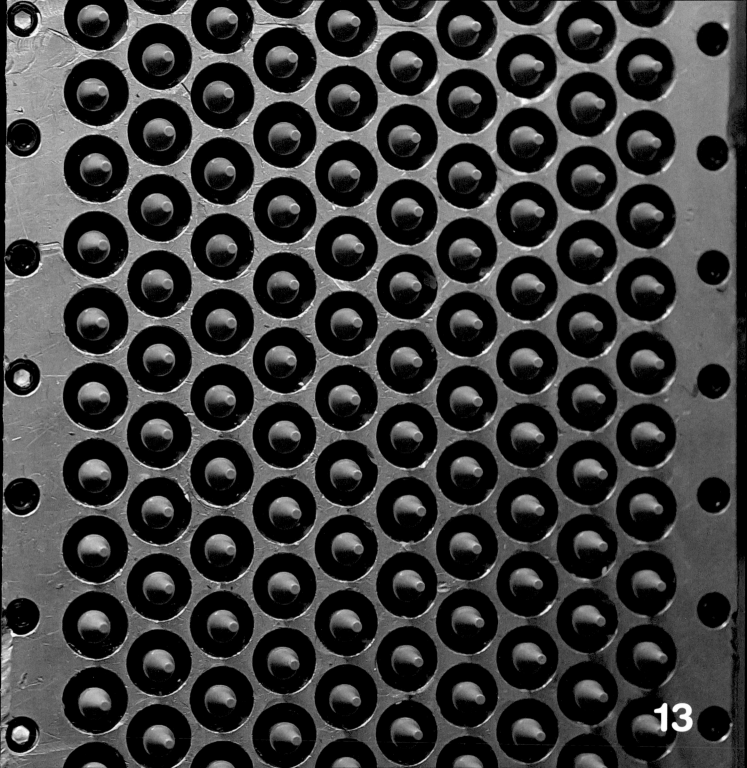

A worker looks at the crayons.

He makes sure the crayons are
not broken.

15

Then, a machine puts **labels** on each crayon.

17

The finished crayons are put into boxes.

Now, the crayons are ready to be used.

We use crayons to draw and color on paper.

Crayons are fun to use.

21

Words to Know

crayons (KRAY–unz) – colored wax sticks used for drawing or coloring

labels (LAY–buhlz) – pieces of paper that are attached to something and give information

melts (MELTS) – when heat makes something change from being solid to being liquid

mold (MOHLD) – a hollow container that you can pour liquid into so that it sets in that shape

powder (POW–dur) – tiny particles of a solid substance

wax (WAKS) – a substance made from fats and oils

Find Out More

Books

How is a Crayon Made?

Oz Charles

Scholastic

What Happens at a Crayon Factory?

Lisa M. Guidone

Gareth Stevens

Website

PBS Kids

Mister Rogers' Neighborhood

pbskids.org/rogers/video_crayons.html

Index